LAST LIGHTS

The Hand-Wound Lighthouses of The Bahama Islands

Annie Potts

fish house press

This book is dedicated to all those who beat to windward.

Copyright © 2011 Annie Potts
*Photographs not by the author are credited and the copyrights
to those photographs remain with their creators.*

Design – Annie Potts

Production – Heidi Rich – richworks graphics – Stuart, Florida

Publisher – Fish House Press – Palm City, Florida – ephemeral@bellsouth.net
a division of Florida Classics Library – P.O. Box 1657, Port Salerno, Florida
floridaclassicslibrary.com

Printer – Southeastern Printing Co., Inc. – Stuart, Florida

Front Cover Photo – "Night Owl, Inagua Lighthouse" © 2010 Annie Potts
Back Cover and page 10 © NASA – The Visible Earth (http://visibleearth.nasa.gov/)
Chart information for pages 4-5 – NOAA, U.S. Dept. of Commerce chart 11013, is in the public domain
Background page 94 – Logbook, *Taria Topan,* Mystic Seaport
Page 94 – various newspaper articles © archives of The New York Times

All rights reserved. No part of this publication may be reproduced, stored in a retrieval system,
or transmitted in any form or by any means, electronic, mechanical, photocopying, recording,
or otherwise, without the prior permission of the publisher.

This book is printed on a 10% post-consumer waste recycled paper with vegetable-based ink
ISBN 978-0-615-47993-4
Library of Congress Control Number 2011929174

Contents

Chart of The Bahama Islands 4

Foreword 7

History 8

Mechanisms and Maintenance 16

The Eleven Manned Lighthouses 50

The Wreck of the *Taria Topan* 92

Keepers' Lives 100

Portfolio 110

Acknowledgements 130

Index 134

Lighthouse Legend

(in chronological order of their construction)

1. HOLE IN THE WALL (Abaco Light Station)

2. GUN CAY

3. ELBOW CAY, CAY SAL (Double-Headed Shot)

4. GREAT ISAAC

5. CAY LOBOS

6. GREAT STIRRUP (Stirrup's Cay)

7. ELBOW REEF (Hope Town)

8. CASTLE ISLAND

9. INAGUA

10. BIRD ROCK

11. SAN SALVADOR (Dixon Hill)

GR FL (5) EV 15 SEC 15 M

Group flashing 5 flashes every 15 seconds, visible for 15 miles. On the deck of our small wooden sailboat, I checked my dimly lit stopwatch and yelled those light characteristics down to the chart table below where, for the first time in a week, I could see my husband's shoulders relax. Finally. The chart showed that the flashes we were seeing intermittently near the horizon were coming from the Elbow Reef Lighthouse (aka the Hope Town Light), Abaco, Bahamas. Gales and confused seas had filled our passage south from North Carolina and grey skies had made noon sights next to impossible. It was 1978. We were young, inexperienced and our navigational equipment was minimal; just an accurate watch and a sextant. This was our first long offshore passage, and after seven days at sea, until seeing those small shafts of light, we were nervous about our location.

With land no higher than 210 feet, fringing reefs and hundreds of square miles of shallow sand banks, the waters of The Bahama Islands are every sailor's nightmare. The complexity of currents and countercurrents, which flow on and off banks, through deep cuts between cays and into deeper channels surrounding them, make passages a challenge.

Most maritime countries have navigational aids such as markers and buoys to guide vessels safely past their shorelines, but The Bahama Islands have few of these. Those that exist are maintained locally and can be very undependable. Here the lighthouses built during the mid-nineteenth century under the direction of the British Imperial Lighthouse Service are the primary man-made structures that signal danger to ships and small craft.

Originally constructed to protect commercial shipping during the rise of international commerce, these eleven light stations still stand. A holdover from another time, they are a tribute to their builders and designers. Ten of these lighthouses currently operate and three of them are still manned, hand-wound and cared for much as they have been for the past 150 years.

FL EV 10 SEC 19 M

One flash every 10 seconds, visible for 19 miles. Several hours later, just before dawn, with Elbow Reef Light astern, we picked up the lume of the Hole in the Wall Lighthouse off of our starboard bow. Easing the sheets, we made our way into the Northeast Providence Channel and safely on to our first visit to Nassau.

History

Viewed from space, The Bahama Banks are quickly identified and it is easy to see a ship's need to avoid them. Here the Atlantic waters form troughs nearly three miles deep as they pass along large island-fringed shallow seas. There are few places on the planet that have such extreme and abrupt changes in water depth. Mariners of the eighteenth and nineteenth centuries with only their shipboard height of eye could not take advantage of a satellite's view. Their pilot books and paper charts were expensive and only available in large cities.

The growth of commercial shipping along the southeastern coast of North America resulted from the geographical expansion of the newly formed United States. The need for lighthouses in The Bahama Islands paralleled this growth. Until the late 1780s, Charleston, South Carolina, had been the most southerly deepwater American port and Tybee Light near Savannah, Georgia, the most southern lighthouse. The Louisiana Purchase of 1803 gained the U.S. a large area of formerly French territories and later, in 1819, the Spanish ceded East Florida to the U.S. These two events added more than 1,800 miles of coastline to the new country and more than doubled the length of the southeastern U.S. coast. By 1820, the ports of New Orleans and Mobile were within U.S. borders. Lumber, cotton, and other goods could now be shipped offshore from the entire length of the Mississippi River. By 1822, Key West, with its well-protected harbor, became America's first recognized seat for the legislation of the legal maritime business of wrecking. Up to that time, the British administered all contested groundings in the area, and legal cases were tried in the courts of Nassau.

In the early part of the 19th century, the United States government contacted the British government concerning the need for light towers along the eastern edge of the Straits of Florida. Safe deepwater routes needed to be established to direct ships into the Gulf of Mexico as well as along the eastern seaboard of the United States. With a prevailing easterly wind and nothing to identify dangerous low-lying islands and sand banks, sailing vessels needed to give shallow water plenty of sea room. The 19th century became the golden age of lighthouse construction.

The Imperial Lighthouse Service, Trinity House, London, built 11 lighthouses in The Bahamas during the 55-year period between 1833 and 1887. By 1833 the British commissioned their first two lighthouses: one at Gun Cay, near Bimini, on the western edge of the Great Bahama Bank; the other at Hole in the Wall, Abaco, on the eastern edge of the Little Bahama Bank. Eight years later they built a third light at North Elbow Cay on the much smaller Cay Sal Bank. This bank stretches along the eastern edge of the of the Straits of Florida and to the west of the Great Bahama Banks. Eight light stations were built at other strategic points where the deep water passages meet the shallow waters of the banks.

As the British Empire spread across the globe, the Imperial Lighthouse Service built hundreds of light towers, for which funding and administration became increasingly difficult. Trinity House tried several systems involving different proportions of home and local involvement but none were successful. One system required a ship to pay fees to any tower it passed by. Those fees would then support the maintenance of that particular tower. But the lighthouses in The Bahamas were remote and used primarily by foreign ships. It was nearly impossible to collect any money for their maintenance.

By 1887, all 11 light stations stood finished. Their locations were chosen intentionally to guide commercial ships away from the shallow banks of The Bahamas by three main routes: one along the east coast of the mainland of Florida and its keys via the Straits of Florida; another between the Great and Little Bahama Banks via the Northeast and Northwest Providence Channels; a third between the Great Bahama Bank and Cuba via either the Crooked or Mayaguana passage and the Old Bahama Channel.

Supplied and maintained on a regular basis, each lighthouse was operated by one to three keepers. Regardless of world wars or other major events that change the pace of life, every one to two hours of every night, of every day, of every year since these towers were erected in the 1800s, someone makes sure their lights shine brightly, protecting the mostly unseen traffic of ships passing silently by.

Hole in the Wall Lighthouse (photograph by John Whiticar)

Dawn over Hope Town from the top of the light tower with Elbow Reef breaking just offshore.

Mechanisms and Maintenance

Over the years, the British Imperial Lighthouse Service continued to make improvements to the range and intensity of their lighthouses' beams. These improvements included changes to their lens and burner designs, fuel sources and rotating mechanisms. The original lights were probably illuminated by vegetable or whale oil lamps with wicks and parabolic reflectors to intensify their beams. The lenses were thick and heavy and rotated very slowly if at all. Though visible at a range of 15 to 20 miles, their beams were weak and ineffective.

THE LENS

In 1822, Augustin Fresnel revolutionized lighthouse technology with his pioneering design of a new type of lens system. Fresnel's innovative lenses consist of hundreds of small glass prisms and lenses that redirect rays from a light source into a more intense single beam. A modular system, these lenses can be constructed, aligned, disassembled and easily shipped to another location for reassembly. Using reflective and refractive elements, they are able to transmit as much as 80 percent of the light from a light source toward an observer, where earlier ones were less than 10 percent efficient. Fresnel lenses were such an improvement over their predecessors that within a few years five companies near Paris were manufacturing their components. Women and children worked at home polishing the finely ground pieces of glass to meet the increased demand for these lenses. Eventually Chance Brothers of England received a license to manufacture them. All the lighthouses in The Bahamas had Chance Brothers Fresnel lenses installed during the major reconstructions in the 1920s and '30s. Only the lighthouses at Elbow Cay in the Abacos, San Salvador and Great Inagua retain these glass lenses.

The first-order, five bull's-eye Fresnel lens at Elbow Reef Lighthouse, Abaco, with its reflecting lenses in the foreground. The lens and its components were manufactured by Chance Brothers, Smethwick, England.

THE ROTATING MECHANISM

Another significant improvement to the lighting of each tower came with the development of the mercury bath gearing system for turning the lens. The large and weighty complex lens floats and rotates on an enclosed trough filled with mercury. Mercury is used because it is more than 10 times denser than water. It provides a smaller, nearly frictionless surface on which the lens can turn.

Using a weight principle similar to that of a grandfather clock, hand-winding these mechanisms every one to two hours provides, through a series of gears, the power to rotate the giant array of lenses. In the case of the Elbow Reef Lighthouse, it takes hoisting 700 pounds of iron weight the height of the tower to turn four tons of lens for two hours.

The bull's-eye portions of the lenses concentrate light rays into a beam. By configuring a different number of bull's-eye sections around the lens's circumference, the lens' rotation creates a sequence of flashes of light unique to each lighthouse.

Elbow Reef Light's round bull's-eye lenses each refract light to make one flash of intense light. The long flat lens reflects light back toward the burner. The rotation of the light's beam might give the impression that the burner itself is moving. In fact, it is the lens itself that is in motion. Note the metal flue and the blue compass rose which attaches to a wind vane on the rooftop of the lighthouse.

The beautiful first-order lens, formerly at Hole in the Wall Lighthouse. In its day, it flashed the characteristics 'one flash, white, every ten seconds' (photograph by John Whiticar)

The double bull's eye lens of the San Salvador Lighthouse on Dixon Hill creates a flashing characteristic of two flashes every ten seconds. *(photograph by Dave Gale)*

The gearing system for turning the seven thousand pounds of glass and metal of the lens at Elbow Reef Lighthouse, Hope Town, Abaco.

Rollers on which the rotating lens revolves on top of the mercury bath trough. *(photograph by John Whiticar)*

Elbow Reef's lantern room has rounded windows and a catwalk above to service the lens. Part of the mercury bath and nearly frictionless revolving lens can be seen in green on the left.

The lantern room houses all the equipment in a huge two-story structure.

It provides enclosed space around the giant lens and an area from which to wind, clean, and service it. There is a small exit doorway in the lantern room's outside wall which allows the keeper access to the narrow exterior walkway called the gallery. From there he can view passing ship traffic. He can also clean the outside of the lantern room's large windows.

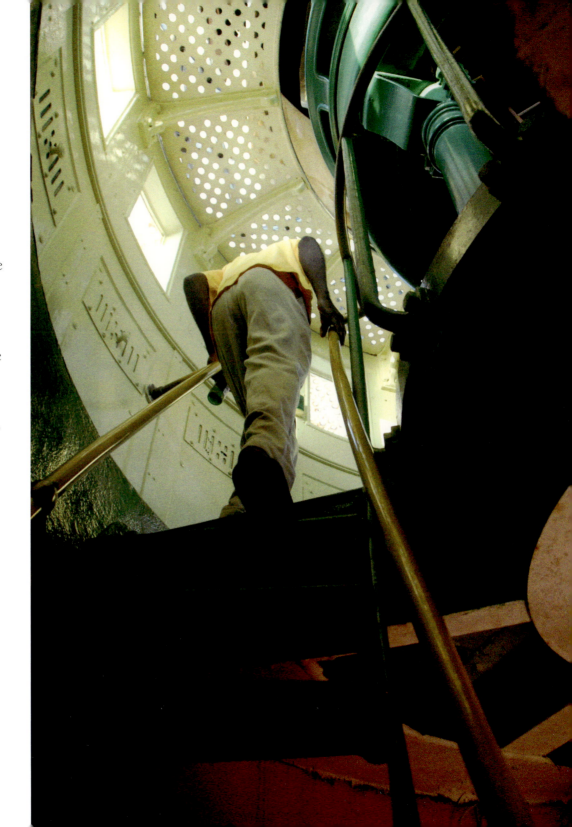

The lantern room at Inagua Light. The service room is the windowless area below the windows. The optic section is the glass area enclosing the lens. Note the grab handles on the mullions for use when cleaning the glass panels. The small gallery door can be seen on the right side of the tower and the canvas covering inside the optic section is also visible.

Lantern room – Elbow Reef Lighthouse. The service room has beautifully curved windows and the glass panels in the optic section are also rounded. The dome above the optic section is vented and contributes to the entire lantern room's ability to draw air up through it like a chimney.

The view northward from the gallery walkway of the Elbow Reef Lighthouse at Hope Town, Abaco. The access doorway is open and its fist-shaped bronze handle is visible.

A look upward in the lantern room at Elbow Reef Lighthouse shows the parts of the sturdy construction of the large lens. Decorative columns support the stationary mercury bath trough. There is a vented metal combing visible on the edge of the rotating lens. The white catwalk and straight green ladders both provide access to the burner.

THE BURNER

The Argand and Fresnel wick burners of the mid-1800s produced small, constant, intense flames, but they did not work particularly well with kerosene. Kerosene burned too richly with most contemporary lamps, a problem that was solved in 1910 with the invention of the Hood Petroleum Vapor Burner. A pressurized kerosene lamp which works much like a modern day Coleman lantern, the PVB burner uses a mantle, produces a more intense light and burns less fuel than the older wick-style lamps. Maintenance records written in 1926 state that all the Bahamian lighthouses had Argand concentric wick burners but were scheduled shortly to receive PVB lamps and the latest lenses. Indeed, these new burners were added during the last major reconstruction of the lights in the early 20th century. However only the lights at Elbow Cay in Abaco and Dixon Hill, San Salvador, continue to use these burners. All the other lights use electricity provided by solar panels or generated by the local power company.

THE FUEL

Trinity House constantly searched for a fuel that would inexpensively burn longer and produce a brighter, more consistent flame. With hundreds of lighthouses throughout the world to administer, controlling the cost of fuel was very important. Equipment costs were also monitored closely. Pieces and parts from lenses, burners, even whole lantern rooms, were sometimes removed and reused as needed in different locations – all in the interest of economically producing the most efficient light source. An example of this thriftiness can be seen today in the fuel tanks at the lighthouse at Hole in the Wall, Abaco. These tanks were originally used at the Eddystone Light in the English Channel and were later shipped to The Bahamas for reuse.

Kerosene became the dominant fuel source by the late 1800s. While the lighthouses in The Bahamas had previously used whale or vegetable oil, other light stations around the world tried different oils including olive oil, shark oil, dolphin oil and lard. Until petrochemicals became popular, colza, an oil from a wild cabbage or rapeseed, had been the most economical and brilliant fuel available. Petroleum or mineral oil, as kerosene was also known, burned brighter than colza and at half the price. It quickly replaced the animal and vegetable oils.

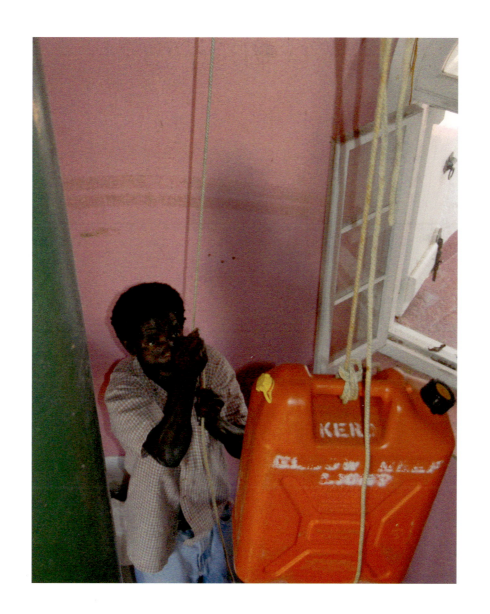

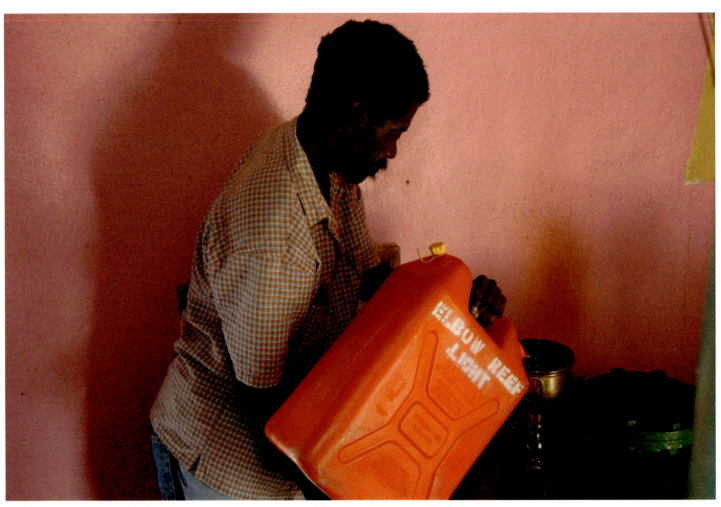
Refueling one of the two large pressurized kerosene tanks which sit on the landing one floor below the lantern room. Only one tank is used at a time. The other is available for backup.

Pumping up the pressure in the kerosene tanks. Each tank is pumped to 80 psi.

Cranking up the weights for the mechanism which turns the lens. Above the hand-crank is a tube through which the mercury can be drained. Every five years it is necessary to clean the inside of the mercury bath trough which rusts and flakes over time.

In the early years, the Imperial Lighthouse Service owned no vessels. It chartered local schooners for the semi-annual inspections and for supplies. Several times the hired crews of these vessels diverted course to salvage cargoes from stranded ships they met along the way. As this behavior was hard to monitor and control, the service eventually acquired a vessel of its own.

The Bahamian light stations, like many others throughout the British Empire, were self-contained outposts. Each had a principal keeper, an assistant keeper and a substitute keeper in case of illness. The keepers made sure all the equipment was kept clean and running. Remarkably, this work was originally inspected only twice a year. At that time the Imperial Lighthouse Service sent a ship from Nassau to each of the light stations. The person hired as inspector was usually an ex-British Navy officer who was very strict about the cleanliness and order of the light stations. One of these men, Commander R. Langton-Jones, held the post from 1929 to 1949 and wrote a book about his years in the Service titled *Silent Sentinels*.

By the mid-1930s the lights at Cay Sal and Gun Cay were no longer manned. Even with only nine stations in full service, it could still take several weeks to make the circuit of manned lighthouses. In preparation for inspection, at each light station, all the brass had to be polished and shining brightly. All lantern room glass had to be clean of salt residue and dirt. The giant lens had to be spotless and the timing characteristics of the light accurate. All the out buildings and residences had to be clean as well. The keepers were fined for anything the inspector found not up to British Navy standard: the white glove standard.

Even so, the keepers celebrated the sight of the lighthouse tender coming over the horizon and into view. The ship's arrival meant not only supplies and stores but also news from the other islands which the inspector served. Passing ships communicated by signal flag and rarely sent anyone ashore. At the lonelier postings, aside from the crew of shipwrecked vessels, the arrival of the inspector might be the only direct contact with life outside the tiny world of the station. Eventually, by the mid 1960s, several stations were routinely visited by fishermen from the United States or Cuba. Radio and television further diminished the isolation.

The Commonwealth of The Bahamas became an independent country in 1973. The new government first supplied these light stations with food once every three months. Finally this service was monthly, although occasionally that one month could grow into three when weather or ship's repairs prolonged the journey. The monthly food supply consisted of three chickens, stew beef, coffee, and pork and beans. Its cost was taken out of the keeper's pay. Since getting provisions ashore to the lighthouse could be very hazardous work in bad weather, all gear and supplies arrived in three large drum-like containers which could be hoisted onto the dock and then rolled up the hill to the light station if necessary. One by one, between 1973 and 1995, the government automated six of the nine lighthouses, dismantling their large Fresnel lenses and the machinery to run them.

Today a keeper's life is still harsh and self-contained. While life in the rest of the world revolves primarily around sunlit hours, it is the keeper's responsibility to man, maintain and clean by hand a complex system of pulleys, gears and fuel that rotates tons of metal and glass throughout the hours of darkness in each 24-hour day.

There is a quiet regular rhythm to each night's work. Climbing the tower; taking down the curtains which during hours of daylight surround the giant lens; priming the vapor burner with alcohol; igniting and setting the pressure of the kerosene which feeds the mantle and fuels the burner; hand winding the cable to the weights that power the gears and rotate the lens; and finally, engaging the gears so that the heavy lens will turn for the next one to two hours. Then descending the tall tower stairs to return again throughout the night to rewind the weights and check how the mantle is burning. In the past, under the British, the principal and assistant keeper would handle alternating two- or even three-hour shifts throughout the night, but now the keepers each do consecutive six-hour shifts.

In contrast to the night's work, each day's effort involves different types of maintenance jobs; cleaning the burners, refueling the kerosene tanks, personal cooking and laundry. With a cistern for water, minimal supplies and only a small cook stove, these jobs are laborious and time consuming. Some days are very busy. Others less so. Light keepers must be inventive and self-sufficient to keep the lights working and have enough food and supplies. And of course, there must be enough time to perfect the fine art of fishing.

Taking down the canvas covering at dusk. Fires have started when the strong Bahamian sunlight has directly hit the prisms in the lens.

Just before lighting the kerosene burner, a small vent which controls the amount of available air is adjusted.

After alcohol has preheated the burner, the valve between the pressurized kerosene tank and the burner is opened and, with a flick of a match, the kerosene becomes vaporized and ignites the mantle.

Ignition. The first moment the burner element is heated sufficiently and the vaporized kerosene begins to burn.

Finally the kerosene burner is lit. The reflection of its intense light is visible in the bull's-eye portions of the lens.

The Eleven Manned Lighthouses

Hole in the Wall Lighthouse *(photograph by John Whiticar)*

HOLE IN THE WALL *(ABACO LIGHT STATION)* – 1836

LAT/LON – 25°51′43″   77°11′59″   FL EV 10 Sec 19M

LOCATION – Southern tip of Great Abaco

HEIGHT OF TOWER – 77 feet   ABOVE HIGH WATER – 168 feet

Although it is close to civilization, Hole in the Wall Lighthouse is reported to have been the most difficult to service. The station takes its name from a large arched opening in the nearby rocky cliffs and is located on an unprotected ironshore-line open to the full force of Atlantic storms and swells. One of the first two towers built by the British, it was the last tower to be automated by the independent Bahamian Government (1995). Until the early 1970s, when a road was cut south from Marsh Harbor, all supplies and personnel arrived at the lighthouse by sea. With that in mind, it is easy to imagine how difficult it was to construct, maintain, and man a lighthouse at this lonely location with the constant roll from offshore swells and salty spray complicating even the easiest tasks.

The original 'Tower of Abaco' was built of local stone and a mortar mixed with brackish water. This mixture never cured completely. Inside this early tower, successive floors of timbers formed a series of rooms connected by wooden stairways. In a document from 1924, it is reported that the old tower was worn beyond repair. That paper describes the light mechanism as *"an old Wilkins Lantern, housing a revolving spindle, on which are mounted a number of 21 inch catoptric reflectors and multi-wick lamps, which revolve by means of a very large old fashioned clock driven by a falling weight at the end of a catgut rope. The light observed from sea is a feeble glimmer and shows a flash at irregular intervals."* Trinity House considered this unacceptable. Because the tower itself was unstable, it was rebuilt to accept *"a first order lantern recently removed from Winterton Lighthouse near Great Yarmouth, the most westerly tip of the British Isles."* This replacement lantern was already 58-years-old, but was of *"thoroughly up to date design and in a sound state of preservation."* To accommodate the additional weight of the lantern, the wooden timbers of the tower were removed and were replaced by a new steel spiral staircase with a stone landing. In the middle of the staircase was a 10-inch diameter steel tube for housing a falling weight system to power the turning mechanism for the Fresnel lens. This rebuilding work began in 1925 and was completed November 5, 1926. Another major reconstruction took place in 1942.

Between 1968 and 1973, Everett Roberts of Green Turtle Cay had the contract with the Imperial Lighthouse Service to provision the nine hand-operated lighthouses at monthly intervals. He recalls his trips to Hole in the Wall Lighthouse as downright treacherous. There were usually large ocean swells running while he was trying to hoist men and heavy materials over his ship's railings to the nearby shoreline. It was precise and dangerous work. He had to position his constantly heaving 100-foot vessel close to the iron shore – but not too close. Remarkably, no one was ever hurt, but many times machinery or full pallets of supplies fell unexpectedly into the sea, rather than making it onto dry land. After the road from Marsh Harbor to Sandy Point was cut through in the 1970s and the spur to Hole in the Wall was added, provisions could be landed at Snake Cay or Marsh Harbor and driven to Hole in the Wall. This made the job of supplying and operating the lighthouse much easier. The bumpy truck ride from Marsh Harbor to Hole in the Wall took well over an hour, but at least it was a dry and relatively safe trip.

When the Bahamian government automated Hole in the Wall Lighthouse in 1995, its unique handmade first-order glass Fresnel lens was dismantled and destroyed. This venerable piece of precision in brass and glass measured over six feet across and weighed more than five tons. It had arrived by sea in many crates from England in the 1920s. Seventy years later it was removed and replaced by a small mass-produced plastic light delivered easily over land.

Hole in the Wall Lighthouse　　　　　　　　　　　　　　　　　　　　(photograph by John Whiticar)

Gun Cay Lighthouse. The base of this tower formerly supported the large first order Fresnel lens which is now atop the tower at Elbow Reef Light, Hope Town. *(photograph by John Whiticar)*

GUN CAY – 1836

Lat/Lon – 25°34′13″ 79°17′51″   FL EV 10 Sec 14M

Location – **Southern end of Gun Cay, Berry Islands**

Height of Tower – **77 feet**   Above High Water – **80 feet**

Because of its location on the westerly edge of the Great Bahama Bank, the light tower at Gun Cay was one of the first two lights constructed. The Straits of Florida are squeezed tightly here between the coast of Florida and the Bahama banks, forcing the northerly set of the Gulf Stream current to increase to speeds of two to four knots. The water in this area of the Straits appears bottomless and has a deep indigo color. It can also be a nasty piece of ocean. Wind from any direction affects the state of the swift current, and seas mount quickly when the wind blows counter to the Gulf Stream. It is no wonder that the governments of the United States and Great Britain wanted lights along this eastern edge of the Straits. Except for Hole in the Wall Lighthouse (1836) all the first four British-built lights are located here on the western edge of the banks.

Gun Cay Light, which at a total height of 77 feet is among the shortest of the light towers, is built of locally-quarried limestone. Construction of the original tower was finished May 13, 1836, followed by a major rebuild in 1929. At its reconstruction the Lighthouse Service installed a first-order Fresnel lens with a candle power of 325,000. Only seven years later, they decided that Gun Cay was no longer an important location for a light station. They carefully disassembled, removed, crated and shipped the entire lantern room to Nassau. Its structure and all machinery were stored until they were shipped to Abaco for reinstallation on top of the Elbow Reef Lighthouse in Hope Town. Gun Cay Lighthouse was first illuminated on May 13, 1836. It was extinguished on May 13, 1936 – 100 years to the day later.

When first built, the Gun Cay Light was described as a white tower with a light which shone every 90 seconds. This station was the first attempt of the British to intervene in the business of shipwrecking and, as a result, the lighthouse at Gun Cay was extremely unpopular with the local wrecking community. By 1872, the tower had been painted red and given a second-order Fresnel lens. A Coast Pilot from 1909 reported the light itself as being red and revolving once every 90 seconds. In 1929, a first-order revolving Fresnel lens group flashing five every 15 seconds was installed. A note from the time written by the Imperial Lighthouse Service, commented that it was very difficult to supply the light keepers with enough good drinking water. The light station was built on a remote cay with no ground water, and the nearby settlers continued to discourage its existence.

Gun Cay Light (photograph by John Whiticar)

Elbow Cay Lighthouse, Cay Sal *(photograph by Kathleen Sullivan-Sealey)*

ELBOW CAY, CAY SAL *(Double-Headed Shot)* – 1839

Lat/Lon – 23°42′   80°24′   Decommissioned 1934

Location – Elbow Cay, Double Headed Shot Cays

Height of Tower – 60 feet   Above High Water – 96 feet

Cay Sal Bank is much smaller and lesser known than the Great and Little Bahama Banks. Its triangular shape forms the northerly boundary of the western end of the Old Bahama Channel. First mapped in 1511 by the Spanish, Ponce de Leon claimed the land for the crown two years later. The bank includes eight named island groups with 96 islands in total, the light tower being on North Elbow Cay in the Double-Headed Shot Cays. The lighthouse at Cay Sal was the third to be completed by the British when it was finished in 1839. It should not be confused with the Elbow Reef Lighthouse in Hope Town, Abaco.

A pilot book from 1909 states that the lighthouse displayed a white fixed light. By 1934, when the tower was closed down, it was described as being painted with red and white stripes. It was only two years later that the light at Gun Cay was decapitated. It was a less important aid to navigation once steam- and gas-powered engines were developed.

During the 1960s and 1970s the Bahamian Defense Force watched for drug trafficking from an outpost set up on the island of Cay Sal which had a small World War II runway. Today the island is also still used by Cubans seeking asylum in the United States. There are many rafts and small boat wrecks on Cay Sal Island, and the lighthouse on Elbow Cay usually has a few jugs of water and some food stashed in the base of the light tower. The tower itself is decorated with the names of many who have attempted the journey from Cuba to freedom by crossing the Gulf Stream. The true number of those who have successfully reached America will never be known.

Great Isaac Lighthouse (photograph by John Whiticar)

GREAT ISAAC – 1859

LAT/LON – 26°1´42˝   79°5´20˝   GP FL (2) EV 10 Sec 23M

LOCATION – 18 miles north of Bimini on the western edge of the Great Bahama Bank

HEIGHT OF TOWER – 137 feet   ABOVE HIGH WATER – 152 feet

Commissioned for the tiny, remote Bahamian cay by that name, Great Isaac Light is among the most famous of the original British built lights. The first lighthouse erected after Victoria became Queen of England, it was inaugurated on August 1, 1859 as the Victoria Light. This new light on Great Isaac Cay was designed and constructed using new technologies and to the highest standard of its day. The tower, made of individual cast iron panels prefabricated in England, was originally assembled in Hyde Park in London as part of the 1851 Great London Exhibition at the Crystal Palace. Chance Brothers of Smethwick, near Birmingham, engineered the lighthouse. Although they had begun as sheet and optical glass makers, Chance Brothers had also become prominent iron forgers and manufacturers of machinery. They took the opportunity to display these combined technologies by featuring Isaac's Light at the grand exhibit at the Crystal Palace.

Isaac Light is impressive with its great height and 13-foot diameter lantern room which encloses a first-order rotating Fresnel lens. After its London debut, the tower was unbolted and shipped aboard the bark *Hero* to Nassau where its pieces were stored until the arrival of the engineer responsible for its reconstruction. Lightering all the equipment onto small Great Isaac's Cay was extremely difficult. In fact, the bark *Stanley*, chartered to deliver the large and weighty pieces of iron, glass and machinery, wrecked in the shallow water just north of the cay while trying to put the materials ashore. She had dragged both of her anchors during a strong norther and was driven onto the off-lying reefs by the onshore winds. The grounding tore a large hole in her hull but did not damage the lighthouse's iron plating stored aboard. All the workmen on the *Stanley* survived, but the ship's cabin boy was washed overboard. While in the water struggling for his life, he was attacked and bitten in half by a shark. The lower half of his body was buried on Great Isaac Cay.

Several ghost stories and tales of disappearances attributed to the Bermuda Triangle have been attached to this lighthouse. One is the story of the Grey Lady. According to the tale, a few years before the lighthouse was erected, fishermen discovered a ship wrecked on Great Isaac Cay. Broken parts of the ship and the mangled bodies of her passengers were found scattered around the cay. Among the bodies was one of a young woman still holding her young infant, who had somehow miraculously survived the maelstrom. The fishermen saved the infant, but since that day reports of a ghostly woman walking around the grounds and up into the tower searching for her child have haunted the island.

The children and wife of Everett Robert posing for their father at Great Isaac Light during a service run. (late 1970s)

A more recent incident occurred in the summer of 1969. In August of that year, the lighthouse was found unmanned. No sign of struggle; all food and gear were accounted for and nothing was missing except the keepers. No additional information about them has ever surfaced. I spoke with a keeper who was in the Lighthouse Service at that time. He felt that the missing men had gone fishing or had tried to make the run to Bimini 18 miles to the south.

So much can happen to a small boat in open water. A few days prior to the disappearance of the two keepers, a hurricane passed through The Bahamas; undoubtedly the seas stayed rough for many days. The same keeper also told me that once while he himself had been stationed at Great Isaac's he had gone fishing in his dinghy and had been unable to row back. A freshening breeze caught him unprepared and blew him more than six miles downwind of the cay. He had given up all hope of being able to row against the strong wind. He was sitting there, alone in his small boat out of sight of land, exhausted, conserving what remained of his energy and courage when a passing yacht spotted him and altered course towards him. Seeing he was in trouble, they threw him a line and towed him slowly back to the cay.

Here is an 1800s photograph taken in London at the base of Great Isaac's lighthouse. Note the numbers on the individual panels – these probably indicate their distinct location for reassembly.

(photographer unknown)

Cay Lobos Lighthouse – Because Cay Lobos is such a tiny island, the light keeper's quarters surround the base of the light tower and provide access to the tower without having to go outside.

(photograph by Dave Gale)

5   CAY LOBOS – 1860

LAT/LON – 22°24˝   77°32´   GR FL (2) EV 20 Sec 21M

LOCATION – Eastern end of the Old Bahama Channel on the southern edge of the Great Bahama Bank

HEIGHT OF TOWER – 145 feet   ABOVE HIGH WATER – 148 feet

Lobos Light sits on a small cay in a lonely part of The Bahamas. It has been called the most picturesque of the light towers commissioned by the Imperial Lighthouse Service. Eighty miles south of Andros Island, its nearest Bahamian neighbor, it is only 17 miles from the coast of Cuba. The light was inaugurated March 31, 1860, less than a year after the completion of Great Isaac light.

Trinity House sent out an English engineer specifically to supervise the construction of this tower as it presented a unique and difficult challenge. Unlike all other Bahamian lighthouses, it is built on sand rather than hard rock. To firmly anchor the structure, very large, heavy teak pilings were driven deep into the sand. The builders then covered that foundation with a 26-foot diameter teak curb. The tower, weighing 230 tons, was built on top of that. It is hard to imagine what methods were used to construct this tower, built 150 years ago without access to modern excavating and building technologies. There is so little solid ground above water on Cay Lobos that the three keepers' residences encircle the base of the tower.

The ten flights (198 steps) up to the lantern room of this tower are steep and challenging. They are accessed directly (without going outside) from the keepers' quarters. When climbed on a clear day, they provide a view of the cays off the north coast of Cuba. To further strengthen the tower, its first 20 feet were filled completely with concrete and passageways were tunneled through it.

This tower and the one at Great Isaac are the only two Bahamian lighthouses that were built of cast iron. This is the only Bahamian lighthouse built on the southern edge of the Great Bahama Bank.

Great Stirrup Lighthouse *(photograph by John Whiticar)*

6 GREAT STIRRUP *(Stirrup's Cay)* – 1863

Lat/Lon – 25°49´23˝   77°54´23˝   GP FL (2) EV 20 Sec 22M

Location – Northern most Berry Island

Height of Tower – 57 feet   Above High Water – 82 feet

Great Stirrup Light was a favorite among those who manned it because it has the shortest tower in the service. It is less than half the height of those at Great Isaac and Cay Lobos. Older keepers would often put in for a transfer to Great Stirrup claiming back problems as their primary reason. Since it was it a shorter climb to the lantern room, it also took fewer cranks to wind the turning mechanism of its large Fresnel lens. However, fewer cranks also meant a shorter time between windings during the long night.

Great Stirrup Cay is at the northeast corner of the Great Bahama Bank and provides a reliable landmark for vessels traveling through the busy channels of Northeast and Northwest Providence Channel. Coming in from the open Atlantic, using Hole in the Wall Light on Great Abaco as a landfall, Great Stirrup is the next light to be identified. Inaugurated May 1, 1863, it was rebuilt in 1928 and 1956, and automated in 1995.

British sailing directions from 1860 described the harbor at Great Stirrup as a perfect location from which to watch for the slavers that frequently passed by. This harbor provides a well-protected anchorage with a shallow bar limiting the draft of ships entering to 12 feet. Union ships looking for blockade runners used the harbor during the American Civil War.

Nassau became a major transshipment port for goods during the American Civil War as the British, though ostensibly neutral, supported the Confederates by allowing their ships to recoal and outfit there. Shipping traffic increased on and around the Bahama Banks during the war, and the lighthouses, offering an accurate known position day and night, alerted ships to shoaling water, saving many of them from unexpected grounding.

Originally, many of the towers were painted red and white to make them more prominent landmarks during the daylight hours.

Hole in the Wall Lighthouse has retained its two-color, red-over-white tower. However, for several decades, Elbow Reef Lighthouse at Hope Town has remained the only 'candy-striped' light.

Castle Island Lighthouse

Cay Lobos Lighthouse with black and white stripes

Great Isaac Lighhouse

(photographs by Everett Roberts)

Great Stirrup's lightkeeper's house *(photograph by John Whiticar)*

Elbow Reef Lighthouse, Hope Town

ELBOW REEF *(Hope Town)* – 1864

Lat/Lon – 26°31´59˝ 76°57´41˝   GR FL 5 EV 15 Sec 15M

Location – Elbow Cay, Abaco

Height of Tower – 89 feet   Above High Water – 120 feet

The best-known and loved lighthouse in The Bahama Islands, the light at Hope Town on Elbow Cay, is a finely preserved example of the lights constructed by the British Imperial Lighthouse Service. Originally built with brick over a form of quarried limestone dug out of the hillside next to the light tower, the Hope Town Light (as it is commonly known) is one of three remaining non-automated lights. The light was probably candle powered and non-rotating until 1938. Its first-order Fresnel lens is now lit with pressurized kerosene and wound by hand.

There was serious opposition to the original building of this lighthouse when it was erected next to a settlement of 550 people, as most of the residents there made their living from wrecking. Before the lighthouse was built, an average of one ship a month wrecked in the Abacos, and many of the people of Hope Town made a good living salvaging their cargoes. The local residents did whatever they could to stall the completion of the lighthouse. They refused food and water to anyone who worked on the tower and outbuildings. They sank barges delivering building materials. But the light was successfully completed in 1863 and has had two major renovations in its lifetime; one in 1938 and another between 1953 and 1955.

As mentioned previously, the British lights along the Straits of Florida became less important in the 20th century than they had been during the 19th century. As sail and steam gave way to fuel oil, ships moved more efficiently. With more sophisticated navigational systems, their courses became more accurate. By the mid 1930s, Cay Sal light had been decommissioned and Gun Cay had been decapitated. The disassembled parts from Gun Cay's lantern were crated and shipped for reinstallation atop the newly reconstructed tower in Hope Town. During this reconstruction a nearby temporary 60-foot light tower was built of 4x4s and 4x6s. A standing flashing light was put in place until everything was ready for the Chance Brothers' Fresnel lens and mechanism. The lighthouse's log reads *"7 November 1937 landed 34 cases of lens and optics."* The light's works were timed on January 14, 1938. Finally on January 31, 1938, the light- as we currently view it- could be seen flashing five bright white flashes every 15 seconds. Apparently the new lighting mechanism required new skills to operate. It was hard to get the timing accurate, and the principal keeper broke his wrist when he first put the new gearing mechanism into motion. The complex lens is 90 inches high with a focal length of 36 inches. It weighs over 7,000 pounds.

The original tower was smooth sided and very graceful to look at with its pale brick covering. Its curved base was designed to take the full force of heavy seas. Unfortunately sea water and local sand were used in its concrete construction. The sand was inferior and the salt in the sea water shortened the life of the iron used for reinforcement. By 1953, the tower needed another major rebuild. Eighteen inches of concrete in successively smaller bands were added to the circumference of the structure. An aggregate of small bluestone, sailed in from Jamaica, made the concrete stronger. Finally, on June 23, 1955, the newly reconstructed lighthouse was completed.

The Elbow Reef Lighthouse is now maintained much as it has been since that day more than 56 years ago. The British government required more from the keepers than the Bahamian government in terms of log keeping, polishing brass and glass and doing yard work. The heavy, multifaceted Fresnel lens revolves nightly in large part due to the hard work of those who constructed it and the loyalty of those who have maintained it through the years. Above all the others in The Bahamas, the Hope Town Lighthouse provides an example of the pinnacle of lighthouse daily life before electricity and plastic. This light and the light at San Salvador may be the only remaining examples in the world of lighthouses that are both hand-wound and use petroleum vapor burners. These last lights have been saved from automation by the Bahamian Lighthouse Preservation Society, a small group of dedicated supporters who, assisting the Bahamian government, continue the hard work of seeing they are kept manned and running.

Uncovering the windows of the Elbow Reef lantern room in preparation for evening.

Castle Island Lighthouse *(photograph by Geoffrey Schultz)*

CASTLE ISLAND – 1868

LAT/LON – 22°7'33"   74°19'41"   GR FL (2) EV 20 Sec 21M

LOCATION – Off the southern tip of Acklins Island on the southeastern edge of the Crooked Island Passage

HEIGHT OF TOWER – 113 feet   ABOVE HIGH WATER – 130 feet

The light at Castle Island shone for the first time in 1868 and marks the narrowest part of the Mira Por Vos Passage, a small passage running between the Crooked Island and Mayaguana Passages. This light originally had a 3-wick lamp before it was upgraded to the PVB burner/Fresnel lens system standard to the Bahamian lighthouses in the 1920s and 1930s. Squiers Brothers, an old Nassau firm, built the tower for a cost of about a 1,000 pounds sterling. Its newer lens was a first-order Fresnel providing 400,000 candle power.

Many ships have wrecked and stranded on the reefs near Castle Island Light. It is a remote and desolate place named for a tiny, white, castle-shaped cay that lies north of the cay the lighthouse sits on and south of the tip of Acklins Island.

In 1908 the British-built steamer *Yumuri*, bound from Jamaica for Baltimore, Maryland with a load of fruit, was disabled and blown ashore on the reefs there. After fighting a hurricane for two days, the *Yumuri* had taken aboard so much green water that her boilers became crippled. Although she stayed afloat, she had no steerage and eventually hit the reefs off Castle Island. The crew survived the grounding, but as the ship continued to break into smaller and smaller pieces, their lives were still in danger. To get ashore through the submerged coral the men were forced to abandon her and travel, half-walking, half-swimming, through the slamming waves. It was a night of horror for them. They suffered multiple cuts and deep wounds. Although no lives were lost, a crew member lost the ship's logbook when it fell from his hands into the surf. Once on land, the men walked two miles to the lighthouse where they were able to get food and water from the light keeper. However, the only shelter he could provide them was in the light tower itself, which at that time was open at the top. One of the crew described their night as similar to one spent sleeping at the bottom of a well. On the following day, the men were rescued by crew from the steamer *Prince Willem,* who rowed their lifeboats until just outside the surf line. They then floated lifelines towards shore and pulled the stranded sailors to safety. With the crew of the *Yumuri* safely aboard, the *Prince Willem* headed for New York City.

The following year, 1909, a British merchant vessel contacted the inspector of the Lighthouse Service in Nassau to say that signal flags indicating *"medical attention urgently needed"* were seen flying from the signal flagpole at Castle Island Light. The vessel stood by and sent a crew member ashore to investigate. The crew discovered that one of the keepers had fallen to his death from the gallery level outside the lantern room. The keeper's remains are now buried on the grounds of the light station.

In 1937, the inspector was again contacted by a vessel that reported the light had been dark for several days. Apparently both keepers had gone fishing in their tender and had unexpectedly been blown far offshore. With no land between them and Europe, they had given themselves up for lost when they were spotted by a large vessel and brought on board. The ship that saved their lives was headed directly for New York City and its captain had no intention of turning back towards Castle Island to drop off the two Bahamian light keepers. This meant that the light remained unlit for a few more weeks. Without it as an aid to navigation, the U.S. cruiser *Omaha* grounded out nearby. When the keepers finally returned from their surprise trip to New York, they were fined a year's salary for their fishing misadventures.

Castle Island Lighthouse (photograph by Geoffrey Schultz)

Inagua Light Station – Matthew Town, Inagua. This station's tower, like the one at Hope Town, has its windows located exactly on the compass cardinals.

INAGUA – 1870

LAT/LON – 20°56´3˝   73°40´25˝   GR FL (2) EV 10 Sec 17M

LOCATION – SW coast of Great Inagua near Matthew Town

HEIGHT OF TOWER – 113 feet   ABOVE HIGH WATER – 130 feet

The light tower at Great Inagua, completed in 1870, is thought to be the finest built in the Service. Originally called the Imperial Lighthouse, its gentle upwardly curving lines are well proportioned and its masonry first quality. Construction was supervised by Howell and Stewart, a New York firm. Between 1850 and 1860, nearly 150,000 pounds sterling of shipping was lost in this area and as a result the towers at Castle Island (1868), Inagua (1870), Bird Rock (1876), and San Salvador (1887) were considered necessary. The Great Inagua Light sits one mile south of the settlement of Matthew Town in the southwestern corner of the island. Local residents of Matthew Town resisted the light tower's construction, just as they had in Hope Town. This would also prove true 15 years later in Cockburn Town, San Salvador, when the San Salvador Lighthouse was being built on Dixon Hill. Salvage was very important to these settlements' economies.

Great Inagua is the third largest island in The Bahamas, and it sits just north of the Windward Passage about 48 miles from Cuba and 60 miles from Haiti. Matthew Town was a very active and important settlement in the later part of the 19th century. During the American Civil War, Union ships would anchor in the area between Great Inagua and Lobos Lights waiting to intercept blockade runners. The Old Bahama Channel is at its narrowest off Cay Lobos where it is only 17 miles between the lighthouse there and the light at Cayo Verde, Cuba. The settlement at Matthew Town, Inagua was the largest community nearby and the lighthouse's location was strategic for trips through either the Windward Passage or the Old Bahama Channel.

Later, with its excellent location relative to steamship line routes, Great Inagua became more important than Nassau for providing crews to the increasing number of ships moving goods to and from Mexico and Central America. The settlement of Matthew Town at that time was large and well laid out with more than 1,500 inhabitants. It even had its own newspaper. Inagua is still a major world supplier of evaporative salt and the site of the world's largest breeding population of the West Indian Flamingo. Now, just as then, the reefs nearby are numerous and treacherous and bear the evidence of many shipwrecks.

Even a small tropical depression can send strong surf ashore at the Inagua Light.

Bird Rock Lighthouse – 1978 *(photograph by John Whiticar)*

BIRD ROCK – 1876

LAT/LON – 22°51.0´   74°22.0´   FL EV 15 Sec 16M

LOCATION – Northeast corner of Crooked Island on the edge of the Crooked Island Passage

HEIGHT OF TOWER – 112 feet   ABOVE HIGH WATER – 120 feet

Bird Rock's unique design has an interesting history. Engineered in 1870 by the head of Trinity House, it was intended for a location at Point Galle in Sri Lanka (Ceylon at that time). The materials for the light were requisitioned. Unexpectedly, the lamp, iron work, lenticular panels and machinery apparently were redirected to their current location on the tiny cay off the northwest corner of Crooked Island. Erected with the oversight of Francis Aranha of Nassau, the light proved much more expensive than expected and took seven years to complete. It was first lit on August 1, 1876.

Bird Rock itself was formerly identified as Passage Islet according to the American Coast Pilot of 1827, presumably because of its location at the southern side of the Crooked Island Passage. By 1860, the Coast Pilot referred to it as Bird Rock. The tiny cay, less than a quarter of a mile long, is only 10 feet above sea level at its summit. The tower is unusual but similar to the light on Cay Lobos because the keepers' quarters flank its base. Here too, there is little room for them elsewhere on the cay. The light tower has six landings with windows and a seventh floor for the lantern room. Its Staffordshire blue brick weathers better than locally-quarried limestone and its tower remained unpainted until after 1955.

When two strong hurricanes (1926 and 1932) swept over the island, all the small wooden outbuildings were washed away. With them went dozens of coconut palms and the six feet of topsoil that once covered the cay. It cost more than 1,700 pounds sterling to repair this damage. New cement buildings, anchored to the rock, replaced those that previously stood on sand.

Bird Rock Lighthouse – 2006

San Salvador Lighthouse – 2005 (photograph by Jerry Rose)

SAN SALVADOR *(Dixon Hill)* – 1887

LAT/LON – 24°5′51″   74°27′11″   GR FL (2) EV 10 Sec 19M

LOCATION – Dixon's Hill, South West Point, San Salvador

HEIGHT OF TOWER – 113 feet   ABOVE HIGH WATER – 160 feet

The light station at Dixon's Hill, San Salvador, was the last of the Imperial Lighthouse Service towers to be built and was inaugurated on April 1, 1887. The history of the island of San Salvador is rich, not only because of the possibility that Columbus landed there, but also because of the large number of plantations established during the late 18th and early 19th centuries. The lighthouse sits high on a windswept hill set back safely from the island's east facing windward coastline and the nearby settlement of United Estates. The graves of Mr. and Mrs. Dixon, who owned the land before the light station was built, have a prominent place within the compound of the station.

Even into the early part of the 20th century, the Bahamian light stations were remote. With no wireless aboard ships and cable offices only available in large cities, communication between ship and lighthouse was still accomplished by flying signal flags.

In 1905, the English owned steamer *Dordogne* was headed for Jamaica when, passing by Dixon Hill Lighthouse, the master noticed signal flags flying. Deciphering the code he read "I am attacked. Want assistance." It was winter and the conditions did not permit the *Dordogne* to stand off the windward coastline of San Salvador to help. So the ship's flagman signaled back, "Will report you at Kingston, Jamaica."

In Kingston two days later, the master's report was cabled to the Governor of the Bahamas. A tender with the inspector and reinforcements set out all the way from Nassau to investigate the situation on San Salvador. All of Nassau waited for their return and report. The incident was even reported in The New York Times, December 31, 1905.

As it turned out, there had been no insurrection. In celebration of the christening of the assistant keeper's newest child, the principal keeper had allowed his subordinate to fly the flags of the young infant's initials from the station's flagpole. The baby's name was Neville Jones, so the flags for "N" and "J" were innocently flown. Flown together in this order, these flags had the more serious meaning when interpreted by the International Code Book of Signals. This was a very expensive mistake for the principal keeper who, although he stood to be fined for the full price of the tender's roundtrip from Nassau, was eventually fined far less.

San Salvador Lighthouse – 1970s *(photograph by Greg Allikas)*

The Wreck of the Taria Topan

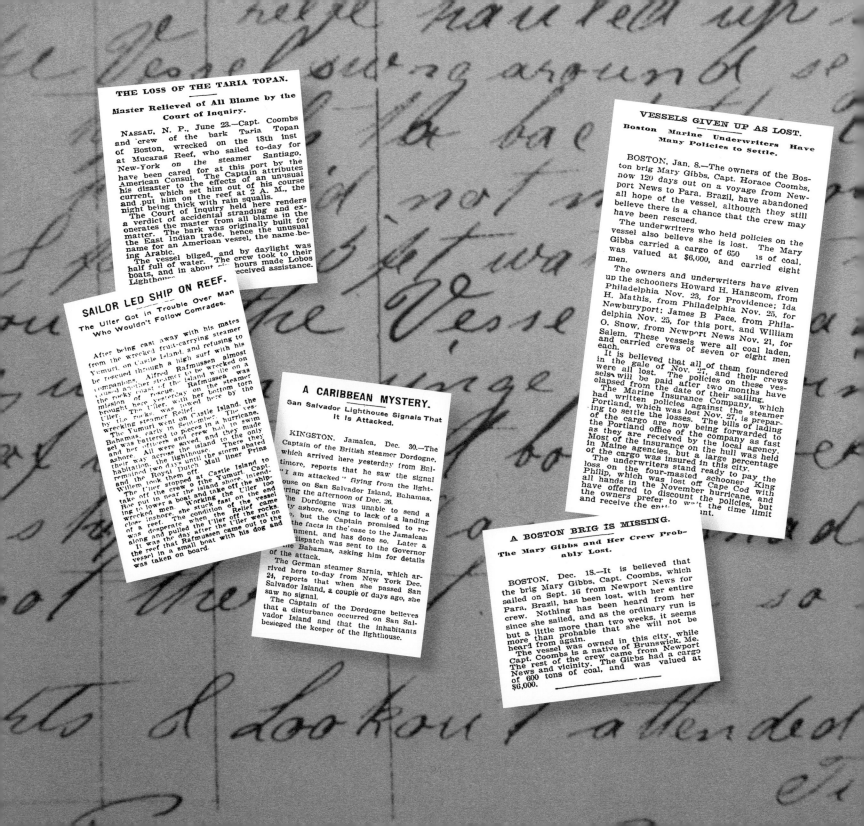

THE LOSS OF THE TARIA TOPAN.

Master Relieved of All Blame by the Court of Inquiry.

NASSAU, N. P., June 23.—Capt. Coombs and crew of the bark Taria Topan of Boston, wrecked on the 18th inst at Mucaras Reef, who sailed to-day for New-York on the steamer Santiago, have been cared for at this port by the American Consul. The Captain attributes his disaster to the effects of an unusual current, which set him out of his course and put him on the reef at 2 A. M., the night being thick with rain squalls.

The Court of Inquiry held here renders a verdict of accidental stranding and exonerates the master from all blame in the matter. The bark was originally built for the East Indian trade, hence the unusual name for an American vessel, the name being Arabic.

The vessel bilged, and by daylight was half full of water. The crew took to their boats, and in about six hours made Lobos Lighthouse, [where they] received assistance.

SAILOR LED SHIP ON REEF.

The Uller Got in Trouble Over Man Who Wouldn't Follow Comrades.

After being cast away with his mates from the wrecked fruit-carrying steamer Yumuri, on Castle Island, and refusing to be rescued through a high surf with his companions, Alfred Rafmussen almost caused another steamer to be wrecked on the rocky coast of the island while on a mission of rescue. Rafmussen was brought here yesterday on the steamer Uller, with her bottom torn by the rocks, was towed here by the wrecking steamer Relief.

The Yumuri went on Castle Island, the Bahamas, early in September. The vessel was battered to pieces in a hurricane, and her officers and crew had to swim ashore. All were saved, and they made their way across the island to the only habitation, the lighthouse. There they remained two days until the storm abated and the Royal Dutch Mail liner Prins Willem took them off.

The Uller stopped at Castle Island to take off the crew of the Yumuri. Capt. Roe put in near the island shore, intending to lower a boat and take off the shipwrecked men. Working the Uller too close inshore, she stuck fast on the end of a reef. The condition of the vessel was desperate when the Relief came along and pulled the Uller off the rocks.

It was the day after the Uller went on the reef that Rafmussen came out to the vessel in a small boat with his dog and was taken on board.

A CARIBBEAN MYSTERY.

San Salvador Lighthouse Signals That It Is Attacked.

KINGSTON, Jamaica, Dec. 30.—The Captain of the British steamer Dordogne, which arrived here yesterday from Baltimore, reports that he saw the signal "I am attacked" flying from the lighthouse on San Salvador Island, Bahamas, during the afternoon of Dec. 26. The Dordogne was unable to send a party ashore, owing to lack of a landing boat, but the Captain promised to report the facts in the case to the Jamaican Government, and has done so. Later a dispatch was sent to the Governor of the Bahamas, asking him for details of the attack.

The German steamer Sarnia, which arrived here to-day from New York Dec. 24, reports that when she passed San Salvador Island, a couple of days ago, she saw no signal.

The Captain of the Dordogne believes that a disturbance occurred on San Salvador Island and that the inhabitants besieged the keeper of the lighthouse.

VESSELS GIVEN UP AS LOST.

Boston Marine Underwriters Have Many Policies to Settle.

BOSTON, Jan. 8.—The owners of the Boston brig Mary Gibbs, Capt. Horace Coombs, now 120 days out on a voyage from Newport News to Para, Brazil, have abandoned all hope of the vessel, although they still believe there is a chance that the crew may have been rescued.

The underwriters who held policies on the vessel also believe she is lost. The Mary Gibbs carried a cargo of 650 tons of coal, was valued at $6,000, and carried eight men.

The owners and underwriters have given up the schooners Howard H. Hanscom, from Philadelphia Nov. 23, for Providence; Ida H. Mathis, from Philadelphia Nov. 25, for Newburyport; James B Pace, from Philadelphia Nov. 25, for this port, and William O. Snow, from Newport News Nov. 21, for Salem. These vessels were all coal laden, and carried crews of seven or eight men each.

It is believed that all of them foundered in the gale of Nov. 27, and their crews were all lost. The policies on these vessels will be paid after two months have elapsed from the date of their sailing.

The Marine Insurance Company, which had written policies against the steamer Portland, which was lost Nov. 27, is preparing to settle the losses. The bills of lading of the cargo are now being forwarded to the Portland office of the company as fast as they are received by the local agency. Most of the insurance on the hull was held in Maine agencies, but a large percentage of the cargo was insured in this city.

The underwriters stand ready to pay the loss on the four-masted schooner King Philip, which was lost off Cape Cod with all hands in the November hurricane, and have offered to discount the policies, but the owners prefer to wait the time limit and receive the entire amount.

A BOSTON BRIG IS MISSING.

The Mary Gibbs and Her Crew Probably Lost.

BOSTON, Dec. 18.—It is believed that the brig Mary Gibbs, Capt. Coombs, which sailed on Sept. 16 from Newport News for Para, Brazil, has been lost, with her entire crew. Nothing has been heard from her since she sailed, and as the ordinary run is but a little more than two weeks, it seems more than probable that she will not be heard from again.

The vessel was owned in this city, while Capt. Coombs is a native of Brunswick, Me. The rest of the crew came from Newport News and vicinity. The Gibbs had a cargo of 600 tons of coal, and was valued at $6,000.

Newspaper articles and logbooks of vessels of the 19th century give a true sense of the great changes occurring in the maritime world of that time. Hand-built wooden sailing ships, slave and spice trading, all major components of the economies of the early 1800s, were no longer standard by the end of the century. The young and growing United States had increasingly changed world commerce with its 'can do' attitudes and appetite for trade. U.S. vessels now routinely traversed the globe trading with Africa, India and Asia as well as delivering goods to and from both coasts of the American continents. Production of goods increased exponentially with the introduction of assembly line methods. Steel and wrought iron replaced wood in ship construction. By 1880, petroleum from Ohio and Pennsylvania shipped through the New York area became the dominant cargo and new industry. At the end of the century, the large handcrafted wooden sailing ships that had spent so much of their time crossing oceans were tired and obsolete. Now they were used mostly for the coastal trade between North and South America. Steam and engine-driven vessels were faster, more dependable and could be handled by a smaller crew.

    I discovered the logbook of the final voyage of the *Taria Topan* in the archives of the Mystic Seaport Museum. I had been poking around, looking for old photographs of the Bahamian lighthouses, when I found her log among many others which had been donated to this New England museum. Rescued well over 100 years ago from the vessel's sinking at Mucaras Reef on the southern edge of the Great Bahama Bank, I wondered how this canvas covered journal had survived its own voyage over the many years and miles it had taken to reach my hands. Reading its handwritten, inked pages I grasped immediately how important the placement of the British-built lighthouses in The Bahamas had been to international shipping under sail. For *Taria Topan*, like many vessels of the time, the shallow banks of the Bahamas had been a navigational nuisance that was difficult to avoid. Days after discovering the logbook, I found a New York Times article from 1896 which gave me a richer perspective on the loss of the ship.

The *Taria Topan* was a 145-foot wooden bark of 631 tons built in 1870 for a wealthy Massachusetts merchant. She had been the star of his fleet and had successfully sailed many lengthy voyages from New England to Zanzibar bringing cotton and, eventually, cheap American kerosene to the east in exchange for spices and ivory. By 1896, she was 26 years old and worn out. Her original owner had died and she was now taking diverse cargo between New England ports, the Gulf Coast and the Caribbean. Having just returned from delivering a load of salt from the Caicos Islands to Providence, Rhode Island, she had again headed south, this time with a load of granite aboard. She had left Rockport, Massachusetts, and was heading for Sabine Pass, Texas.

Today's fast-moving freighters with sophisticated navigational gear can safely navigate this route by heading directly south from New England, staying along the east coast of the United States through the Straits of Florida and then rounding the Florida Keys into the Gulf of Mexico. That passage was slow and potentially dangerous for the sailing vessels of the 19th century because they would be bucking the strong northerly setting current of the Gulf Stream with only the uncertain wind for their power.

At first I was surprised to read in the U.S. Coast Pilot of 1877 that a vessel headed south from New England to a port in the Gulf of Mexico was instructed to sail east of The Bahamas and then fall off to the southwest and pass through the islands using either the Crooked Island or Mayaguana Passage. Either of these two channels provide a deepwater route to reach the easterly end of the Old Bahama Channel. Piloting a vessel via this route does enable a ship to pass safely south of the Great Bahama Bank and, with a favorable course to wind, use the aid of the carefully positioned Cuban lighthouses for navigation. This route also avoids the Straits of Florida and the Gulf Stream. However, it is considerably longer and has its own hazards.

According to her log, the *Taria Topan* began her trip from Massachusetts in good weather. Some days she clipped along covering more than 170 miles, while others she wallowed at a mere 22. She left Bayview, Rockport, Massachusetts, on May 29. More than two and a half weeks passed before she saw her next land, an island in the southeastern Bahamas. The winds were mostly easterly and southeasterly. The air must have been warm. Going aloft to reef or shake out the square sails required a big effort for her crew. Her log doesn't give much detail about the passage except to give assurance to its reader *"all pumps, lights, and lookouts attended to."*

"Noon, Mayaguana Island bore SE distance 7 miles" the mate wrote in his noon entry on June 17. He recorded that the ship had sailed 177 miles that day. By 8 p.m. on that night, he reported the *Taria Topan* was off the southern tip of Acklins Island and the lookout had picked up the lume of Castle Island Lighthouse. By 11p.m. the mate logged that light as bearing north at a distance of eight miles. A light rain had begun to fall. By the middle of the next day, June 18, Cay San Domingo on the southern edge of the Great Bahama Bank bore north at three miles and the ship had successfully passed into the Old Bahama Channel.

A close look at the chart shows how the eastern end of the Old Bahama Channel becomes quite narrow before it widens again east of Cay Sal Bank. The several lighthouses along the northern coast of Cuba delineate the southern edge of the Old Bahama Channel, but only the lighthouse at Cay Lobos marks the scalloping southern edge of the Great Bahama Bank and the shallow water to the north.

Today's seamen receive constantly updated real-time information of their location from global positioning equipment. At any time of day or night the crew can electronically locate their vessel to within 100 feet. However even today, as a 21st-century mariner will tell you, the way to confirm a ship's exact position definitively as it is nearing land is to visually verify its location relative to a known shoreside object.

During the 19th century, a good sextant, chronometer and taffrail log were the only instruments available for calculating a ship's position while out of sight of land. Sextant sights could be taken at noon or night, but only if the weather was cooperative and the sun and stars were visible. When daily sextant sights were not possible, the navigator could only advance his position along his charted course line by multiplying his boat speed per hour by the number of hours he'd traveled since his last sextant shot.

There are strong currents on and off the shallow banks in The Bahamas, the direction and strength of which sometimes up to 4 or 5 knots have always been hard to measure. Out of sight of land, the true effect of these currents on ships passing through the islands is difficult to establish. A good lookout posted at all times was essential to a safe passage for the *Taria Topan*. Her true speed and direction over the bottom could be very different from her one through the water, and, as a result, her real location was difficult to establish accurately. The New York Times article quotes the captain of the *Taria Topan* as stating that the current and weather caused him to wreck his vessel on the Great Bahama Bank.

The mate's final entry in the logbook dated June 18, 1896, reads:

> *Towards midnight rain squally and thick weather. At 2:15 vessel struck on reef. Hauled up all sails. The vessel swung around. Set main topsails*
>
> *Tried to back the vessel off but did not move. Sounded pumps and found 5 feet of water in the hole. At daybreak we found the vessel breaking up so fast that there was no saving her she being half full of water got boats over and made ready to leave the ship at 10 am made for Lobos light and got there at 4*
>
> *So I end my log-pumps lights and lookout attended to at all times*
>
> – P. Petersen, mate

The logbook ends with a sworn statement from the mate that his log is a true and accurate account of the voyage and grounding. It is signed and stamped June 20, 1896 by the United States Consulate, Nassau, New Providence.

In September of 1898, Captain H.R. Coombs who had been the last skipper of the *Taria Topan*, had become the captain of the brig *Mary Gibbs*. The *Gibbs* left Newport News that month carrying a load of coal to Pema, Brazil. She was reported overdue two months later and presumed lost. Nothing was heard of her or her crew again.

Keepers' Lives

Wilfred Wilson was born in 1954 and has spent most of his life on the island of Inagua. He had worked for 16 years as a welder for Morton Salt in their evaporative salt works when his eyes started to fail from the bright light, and he applied to the Port Department in Nassau for the principal keeper's position at the light station on Inagua. He worked there with an assistant for several years until his coworker had health problems and was unable to continue with his job. Now Keeper Wilson operates the tower for the entire night by himself. He is a peaceful and quiet person to spend time with and we enjoyed each other's company. As we sat one evening under the turning lens, our conversation was low and the steady clink, clink, clink from the interlocking gears added to the night's harmony. He said he enjoyed his work but that staying awake for the whole night was hard on him. He is in his fifties and in very good shape physically. His nightly duties of winding up the weights every hour and a half have left his body well toned, although he admits he cranks the mechanism's handle slowly and steadily to minimize pressure on his shoulder. He is married and his wife and granddaughter take care of him during daylight hours. He has now worked for the Port Department for more than 10 years. Doing his job alone is hard work.

Keeper Wilson takes his job seriously. The lantern room is orderly. The brass works are all polished and the lens is clean. He uses Windex to clean the glass and Brasso to clean the brass. The lantern room's lenticular panels are without cracks and he told me the tower doesn't leak, although he pointed to the joint between the roof and the walls of the lantern room and said that workmen had recently sealed it and stopped it from leaking.

Mr. Wilson was at the Inagua Station in September 2008 when Hurricane Ike passed directly over. He was in the light tower when the full force of the storm hit. Each pounding wave shook the buildings, and large waves came ashore beyond the tower and inland towards the keepers' houses. However it remained dry within the lighthouse. When the thunder and lightning began, Wilson became afraid to stay up in the tower, the tallest structure in the area, and he headed down from the lantern room. At that point, a bolt of lightning hit the tower. He could feel the electrical charge, but since he was standing on the wooden treads of the spiral staircase, the charge dissipated around him and he descended safely. This strong hurricane caused major damage on Great Inagua. Four years later, although most of Matthew Town has recovered from the hurricane, there are still many houses and churches in need of reconstruction.

Mr. Wilson enjoys his job even if it is lonely at times. He watches television and sometimes goes out on the gallery and watches the stars, the lights of Matthew Town, or the cruise ships filing by on their way back towards Nassau. It is hard for him to be awake while most of the world sleeps, but that is the compromise he must make.

About 10 years ago, it became difficult for the Inagua light keepers to acquire enough kerosene for the light tower. Even though the burner uses less than two gallons of fuel per night, the Bahamian government was unable to provide the station with a steady source of clean fuel. At that point, a 1,000 watt electric bulb was incorporated into the burner system. The Inagua Light again shines two flashes every eight seconds. I have been told that its lume can be seen 27 miles out to sea; 10 miles beyond what it had previously with its Petroleum Vapour Burner.

During Keeper Wilson's tenure, the main gear on the lens's rotating mechanism became badly bent. He feels that perhaps this was because the mechanism's aging cables had snapped several times over the years allowing the weights to crash. The strain exerted when the weights landed could have eventually caused the main gear to deform. Even with the help of Morton Salt's facility on Inagua, it took more than six months for a replacement gear to be made. During this time the light was lit but did not rotate. The cables are now covered with a plastic coating and kept well greased. This is the only time in more than 100 years that a gear to the mechanism had failed.

Presently the Inagua Light's primary use is to guide cruise ships and tankers through the Windward Passage and small Haitian freighters and sailboats from Hispaniola past the shallow waters of Great Inagua. While it may be merely an aid to navigation for the larger ships, Inagua Light is truly a lifesaver to the Haitian boats as the sea continues to regularly claim these crudely-built vessels. The long nights that Keeper Wilson spends winding the turning mechanism for the lens have thankfully prevented this from happening near Inagua during his watch.

Many lighthouse keepers speak of having a special intimate feeling for their light station.
Wilfred Wilson – Principal keeper, Inagua Light Station

Franklin Sweeting – The bad weather that had chased us to the west on our attempted trip to the Caribbean so many years ago became our good fortune when we sailed into Nassau Harbor and first enjoyed the kindness of the Bahamian people. Potter's Cay in the 1970s was a bustle of conch fishermen, long-distance sailors and all types of water people and craft. Experiencing the waterfront as it was then helped me begin to understand the lives of the Bahamian people who survive very simply in a country which has more miles of water than it does acres of land. Thirty years of change has made many of these places and people unrecognizable. However, spending part of each year in The Bahamas has helped make these differences seem less extreme.

I met Franklin Sweeting, principal keeper at the Elbow Reef Light Station, years after that first long passage to Nassau, but getting to know him reminded me of those early days where, even in an active city, the pace of life along the harbor was slow and hours were still considered productive if merely spent in conversations on the subtleties of the weather or the remarkable behavior of fish. Over the few years when I came to know him, we spent a good deal of time talking, or not, appreciating the silence and the beautiful view from the light station eastward to the settlement of Hope Town and beyond. He spoke slowly with a polite island manner, quiet and direct as a fresh morning breeze.

Keeper Sweeting was born in 1954 in Kemp's Bay, Andros, and moved to Nassau at a young age. He was only a teenager when he applied for a job with the Lighthouse Service. He told me he liked the idea of the quiet work and had no problem with the thought of working nights. He had found life in Nassau had all the temptations of any large city and reasoned that leaving that world behind might be good for him. After passing an admission exam that required both a math test and a physical exam, he was sent out to Bird Rock Lighthouse off Crooked Island for a month's training. There he apprenticed under Principal Keeper Rudie Gibson who showed him onsite the requirements for the standard daily routine at a Bahamian light station. In March 1972, he was given his first posting to Hope Town where he served as relief for a vacationing keeper.

While I had imagined that each keeper would have been assigned to a particular lighthouse to which he would be attached throughout his career, I learned this was not so. For reasons of health, vacation leave, personality conflicts or insubordination, keepers shifted irregularly and often between the nine manned lights. Franklin's first posting at the Elbow Reef Lighthouse was for 10 months, after which he moved to Hole in the Wall, Great Isaac and San Salvador. Over his career he worked at every one of the manned lighthouses except Castle Island. When Cay Lobos and Great Isaac were automated in 1984, he was there to close each of them down. At that point the service began to intermittently station some of the keepers at Nassau Harbor Control, rotating them between there and out in the field as needed.

Franklin shared with me some of his lifetime of experiences in the light stations of The Bahamas. Many times we would talk until the late afternoon light faded and it was time for him to begin his evening duties. Talking together in this setting put me in touch with the life he had lived in these distant outposts. Climbing the tower with him, following his slow, deliberate pace and listening to the wind rattle the shutter hinges, I could have been at Great Isaac, Cay Lobos or any of the more remote, hard rock towers. Although his work was repetitive and his life had been hard, he seemed to have something good to say about most of the light stations. While Cay Lobos was a tiny island far from the other Bahamian islands, he said the fishing was wonderful and the conching even better. Cubans would visit there occasionally, and he had found that it wasn't as lonely as one might think. Stirrup Cay's tower was so short one could almost jump out the top window and operating it did not involve a long climb up hundreds of steep steps. Elbow Reef, San Salvador and Inagua Lights were in or near settlements so they were comfortable postings. Hole in the Wall was difficult because of its isolation. While he had worked there, one of the other keepers disappeared and was later found dead. This keeper had wandered off in the heat of a summer's day and did not return to the station that evening. Days passed before his body was located in a small sink hole in the bush. Franklin mentioned to me that this sad experience was one he will never forget.

In September 1999, category 4 Hurricane Floyd hit the Abacos. Franklin told me that he had been on duty during the worst of the storm and had had to haul his way along the hurricane rails to get from his quarters to the light tower. The full force of the storm hit as he reached the lantern room. By then it was raining so hard through the lantern room windows that he had tried to sleep standing up. He stayed upright throughout the entire dark night, and it had not even been possible for him to wind the mechanism. Although the keepers's houses were severely damaged, the tower itself stood up despite rumors that circulated around the islands saying that it had fallen over. I thought of the isolation and sense of responsibility he must have felt during those long, dark, wet hours. The view from the tower the morning after the storm passed through must have been devastating.

Franklin spent six years at the Inagua light before returning to Hope Town for this his final posting. He was there, in Inagua, when the change from kerosene to electricity was made.

With only three manned towers, the Port Department has less need of lightkeepers. Although Franklin is fairly fit from the exercise involved in his nightly routine, he will have to retire soon. Hopefully a new keeper can be found to replace him. It may be impossible to find someone with the experience he has brought to the job. With luck, someone can be found with the same dedication.

Franklin Sweeting – lightkeeper, Elbow Reef Light, Hope Town, Abaco

Portfolio

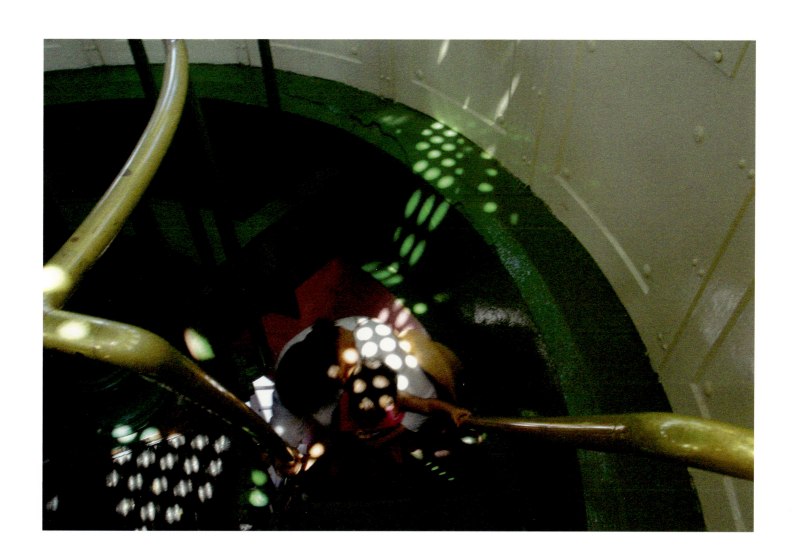

There seems to be little in the 21st century to convince us of the need to continue to hand operate these beautiful structures. Signal flags have given way to wireless radio and cell phones; kerosene and revolving glass lenses to small plastic ones with solar panels. Aboard ship, sextants and chronometers have been replaced by Global Positioning Systems. Only as we imagine the world in which these objects were necessary can we gain perspective on the decision of the British government to expend huge amounts of energy, money, and time in the design and construction of these light stations. Today we can only fantasize about the lives lived within the walls of the towers and keepers' houses, the long hours of boredom punctuated by brief episodes of terror and heroism. But by seeing life as it remains in the last three hand-wound stations and spending time with their keepers, the last in a long line of men who have kept their lamps burning, we are reconnected to a sense of wonder. The more we take the time to study and understand the engineering details of these light stations- their complex simplicity- the more they speak to us and force us to refocus our minds more intently on life all around us. In this way they continue to be beacons of light, but now it is to us they are quietly signaling, warning us to avoid the shallow waters of our own complacency.

The small mantle to the stationary pressurized kerosene burner is accurately placed at a precise distance from, and height within the rotating lens.

Tons of beautiful rotating brass and glass have been replaced with a variety of lightweight plastics to light the solar-powered towers.

(photograph by Dave Gale)

Acknowledgements

The Bahamas is a country of contrasts; wild, yet civilized; remote, yet close to Florida. It is a well-known country and yet it is full of mystery. This book is a product of my love for these islands and their history, and my passion for sailing among them. Traveling by sail, at less than 6 knots, staying in remote places until chased away by weather or called elsewhere by the muse, cameras and my own logbooks, have been my means of connecting with a life that would have been difficult to understand had I been moving more quickly. And it would have been impossible without the openness of the Bahamian people who are among the most warm-hearted on the planet.

I am grateful to the many people who helped me with this book; the other photographers, especially John Whiticar, who shared their work and all who helped with the editing, printing, and publishing process. I thank the Bahamian government who continues to maintain these lighthouses, and keepers Franklin Sweeting and Wilfred Wilson who patiently answered my many, many questions. Very special thanks go to Dave Gale and Jerry Whiteleather of the Bahamas Lighthouse Preservation Society whose quiet efforts and combined abilities have been responsible for overseeing the maintenance and repair of the last three manned light stations.

At this time, it is uncertain whether these last lights will be able to escape automation. Still powered by keepers and kerosene, they are the last of their kind in the world. I hope this book will help to keep them as they are – unique, mechanical wonders with the touch of humanity we all crave.

Dave Gale   *(photographer unknown)*

On location – Ship Channel Cay, Exuma

About the Author

Annie Potts has lived on or near the water all of her life. She has been sailing from the time she could walk. The fourth child of a family with a long and rich maritime history, she uses photography and writing to portray her passion for exploring the triumph of the human spirit and for revealing the interplay between human and natural elements. She presently lives in southeast Florida. This is her first book.

(photograph of author by Tom Zydler)

Index

Abaco Light Station, 4, 53
Acklins Island, 77, 97
American Civil War, 69-70, 81
American Coast Pilot, 85
Andros Island, 67
Aranha, Francis, 85
Augustin Fresnel, 18
Bahamas Lighthouse Preservation Society, 133
Bahamian Defense Force, 61
Berry Islands, 57
Bimini, 12, 63-64
Bird Rock Lighthouse, 4, 81, 84-85, 87, 106
British Imperial Lighthouse Service, 7, 73
Castle Island Lighthouse, 4, 70, 76-79, 81, 97, 107
Cay Lobos Lighthouse, 4, 66-67, 70
Cay Sal, 4, 12, 39, 60-61, 73, 97
Cay Sal Bank, 12, 61, 97
Cay Sal Island, 61

Cay San Domingo, 97
Cayo Verde, 81
Chance Brothers, 18-19, 63, 74
Chance Brothers Fresnel, 18, 74
Cockburn Town, 81
Commonwealth of The Bahamas, 42
Coombs, Captain H. R., 98
Crooked Island, 77, 85, 96, 106
Crooked Island Passage, 77, 85
Crystal Palace, 63
Cuba, 12, 42, 61, 67, 81, 97
Dixon Hill Lighthouse, 89
Dordogne, 89
Double-Headed Shot Cays, 61
Eddystone Light, 32
Elbow Cay Lighthouse, 4, 12, 18, 32, 60-61, 73
Elbow Reef Lighthouse, 4, 7, 15, 19-21, 24, 26, 29-31, 56-57, 61, 70, 72-75, 106-107, 109

Fresnel lens, 19, 54, 56-58, 63, 69, 73-74, 77,
Gale, Dave, 23, 66, 129, 133-134
Global Positioning System, 126
Great Abaco, 53, 69
Great Bahama Bank, 12, 57, 63, 67, 69, 95-98
Great Inagua, 18, 81-82, 103-104
Great Isaac Cay, 4, 62-65, 69, 107
Great London Exhibition, 63
Great Stirrup Lighthouse, 4, 68-71
Great Yarmouth, 53
Greg Allikas, 91
Gulf of Mexico, 11, 96
Gulf Stream, 57, 61, 96
Gun Cay Lighthouse, 4, 56-59
Haiti, 81
Hispaniola, 104
Hole in the Wall Lighthouse, 4, 7, 12, 13, 22, 52-55, 57, 69, 70, 107
Hood Petroleum Vapor Burner, 32

Hope Town Light, 7, 73
Hurricane Floyd, 108
Hurricane Ike, 103
Imperial Lighthouse Service, 7, 12, 18, 39, 54, 58, 67, 73, 89, 134-135
Inagua Lighthouse, 4, 28, 80-81, 83, 103-105, 108
International Code Book of Signals, 90
Jamaica, 74, 77, 89
Jones, Neville, 90
Key West, 11
Langton-Jones, Commander R., 39
Little Bahama Bank, 12
Lobos Light, 67, 98
Louisiana Purchase, 11
Marsh Harbor, 53-54
Matthew Town, 80-82, 103
Mayaguana Island, 97
Mayaguana Passage, 12, 96
Mercury, 20, 25-26, 31, 38

Mira Por Vos Passage, 77
Morton Salt, 102, 104
Mucaras Reef, 95
Mystic Seaport Museum, 95
Nassau Harbor, 106-107
North Elbow Cay, 12, 61
Northeast Providence Channel, 7
Northwest Providence Channel, 69
Old Bahama Channel, 12, 61, 67, 81, 96-97,
Paris, 18
Passage Islet, 85
Petersen, P., 98
Petroleum Vapour Burner, 103
Port Department, 102, 108
Prince Willem, 78
Roberts, Everett, 54, 70
Rose, Jerry, 88
San Salvador Lighthouse, 4, 23, 81, 88, 91
Schultz, Geoffrey, 76, 79
Silent Sentinels, 39

Snake Cay, 54
Squiers Brothers, 77
Stirrup Cay, 4, 69, 107
Straits of Florida, 11-12, 57, 73, 96
Sullivan-Sealey, Kathleen, 60
Sweeting, Franklin, 106, 109, 133
Taria Topan, 3, 92, 95-98
Tower of Abaco, 53
Trinity House, 12, 32, 53, 67, 85
Tybee Light, 11
United Estates, 89
Whiteleather, Jerry, 133
Whiticar, John, 13, 22, 25, 52, 55, 56, 59, 62, 68, 71, 84, 132
Wilson, Wilfred, 102, 105, 133
Windward Passage, 81, 104
Yumuri, 77-78
Zanzibar, 96
Zydler, Tom, 133